Science Homework for Key Stage 2

Science Homework for Key Stage 2

Activity-based learning

Colin Forster, Vicki Parfitt and Andrea McGowan

Illustrated by David Brookes

First published 2010
by Routledge
2 Park Square, Milton Park, Abingdon, Oxon OX14 4RN

Simultaneously published in the USA and Canada
by Routledge
270 Madison Ave, New York, NY 10016

Routledge is an imprint of the Taylor & Francis Group, an informa business

Typeset in Frutiger and Sassoon by Wearset Ltd
Printed and bound in Great Britain by MPG Books Group, UK

British Library Cataloguing in Publication Data
A catalogue record for this book is available from the British Library

Library of Congress Cataloging in Publication Data
Forster, Colin.
   Science homework for key stage 2 : activity-based learning /
Colin Forster, Vicki Parfitt and Andrea McGowan; illustrated by
David Brookes.
      p. cm.
   1. Science—Study and teaching (Elementary)—Activity
programs—Great Britain. 2. Homework—Great Britain.
3. Education, Elementary—Parent participation—Great Britain.
4. Active learning—Great Britain. I. Parfitt, Vicki. II. McGowan,
Andrea. III. Title. IV. Title: Science homework for key stage two.
   LB1585.5.G7F67 2010
   372.3'5044—dc22   2009010079

ISBN10: 0-415-47454-X (pbk)
ISBN10: 0-203-87103-0 (ebk)

ISBN13: 978-0-415-47454-2 (pbk)
ISBN13: 978-0-203-87103-4 (ebk)

To GB.
Thank you.

Contents

Materials and their properties

Physical processes

Guidance for the teacher: how to use this 'pencil-free' homework book

Introduction

Many primary school teachers feel frustrated when they find themselves setting homework that they know isn't helping the children with their learning. Maybe the tasks are boring, poorly matched to the children's abilities, and too worksheet oriented. Maybe they know the tasks do nothing to reinforce learning, but instead reinforce negative feelings about learning. Many teachers feel frustrated that setting, collecting and marking homework is a chore with little return in terms of children's learning. Too often homework can become a site of tension between teachers and children and between teachers and parents, not to mention between children and parents, and the home–school partnership is diminished, not strengthened.

Science Homework for Key Stage 2 is a resource that aims to make homework a more positive experience for all concerned, especially children.

Pedagogy and philosophy

Primary school teachers know that children learn through doing and that talking about their experiences is a crucial part of the learning process, as it enables children to revisit and reinforce ideas by reworking them in their own words. However, for many children, homework has become synonymous with 'doing the worksheet' and for many parents, homework is about 'getting the sheet done'.

Science Homework for Key Stage 2 provides good opportunities for learning through doing and for parents/carers to talk with the children about their ideas to share in the learning. *Science Homework for Key Stage 2* enables teachers to set homework that they feel is learning-focused, rather than task-focused, and helps foster positive relationships between all members of the school community.

Science Homework for Key Stage 2: the key ideas

- *Science Homework for Key Stage 2* is pencil-free; the homework sheets are not worksheets – there is nothing for the child to 'fill in'.
- Parents and carers are encouraged to share the homework with the child through activity and discussion (but it doesn't just have to be parents – it could be anyone in the family or household).

- The activities are done with items and materials found in the home, and have a focus on discussion.
- Since there is nothing for the child to fill in on the sheet, there is nothing for the teacher to collect and mark, but there will be lots to talk about in a follow-up discussion.
- The homework is arranged in topics to correspond to the QCA scheme of work.
- There is a blank template on page xiv for teachers to use to devise their own homework activities to allow for further creativity and development.

Following-up on the homework

Whether you select a homework that follows up on work done in class or that introduces a new idea, it is important to follow it up with a class-based discussion about the homework. It would be valuable to find out how the children got on, what they learnt, whether their parents or carers learnt anything and if they raised any good questions about the topic. In this way, it is clear that homework is not a stand-alone activity, but part of a learning process that combines both home and school experiences.

Possible follow-up activities

- Class discussion, with the children reporting on how they got on, and what they found out.
- Class discussion, with the children sharing any questions they raised while doing the activities.
- Group discussions, with each group deciding the most important things they found out.
- Group discussions, with each group deciding which is their favourite question from the ones they all raised.
- Group presentation based on their homework.

Partnership with parents

It is important to keep parents informed of the purpose of the homework and their role in their children's learning. We have provided a draft letter that might be used each term to remind them of the approach taken in *Science Homework for Key Stage 2*. You may like to use a home–school book for parents to provide some feedback on how they and their children got on with the homework.

Template letter

Dear Parent/Carer

Science homework this term

Our science topic this term is _____ and we will be exploring the following ideas:

-
-
-

The science homework we will be giving on this topic will aim to reinforce these ideas through **doing** and **talking**; we will not be asking the children to fill in a worksheet for their homework as we don't believe this will help them learn.

Why doing and talking? Children learn much more by telling other people about their understanding than they do by being 'told' stuff, and doing active tasks gives them lots to talk about and provides experiences to reflect on.

It's not just good for children: Parents and carers often don't get to hear much from their children about what they're doing at school, and sharing a discussion is a good way to find out how much your children are learning.

Another advantage: Homework can sometimes become a battleground; we hope children will need less nagging to do this homework and that they, and you, will learn a lot from doing it, and possibly even enjoy some of it.

Feedback to the school: Please let us know how you and your child get on with the tasks. It would be useful for us to know if your child grasped the ideas well or explained them clearly or if they learnt anything from doing the activities. You might also like to give us some feedback on whether they enjoyed the tasks.

How the school will follow-up the homework: Your child's teacher will organise a time for the children to discuss and share their experiences of doing the activities. This will give the children the chance to reinforce their learning and for the teacher to assess their progress.

Blank active homework template

Aim of the activity

-
-
-

 Think about and discuss

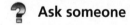 Ask someone

 Tell someone

Life and living processes

Teeth and eating: types of teeth

Look at your teeth in a mirror; feel the shape of each one with your tongue.

Think about and discuss

Think about the size and shape of each tooth and what each one does when you eat. If it helps you to think about it, eat something healthy and think about how different teeth are doing different jobs.

Show someone else your teeth and describe what they do.

During a meal, count how many times you need to chew different kinds of food. Compare your results with someone else.

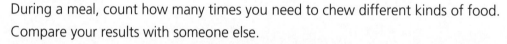

Think about and discuss

Why do you need to chew your food?

Teeth and eating: looking after your teeth

Aim of the activity

- To think about how to look after your teeth.

Time yourself brushing your teeth. How long does it take?

Think about and discuss

Think about how your toothbrush works and what jobs it has to do.

Invent an improvement to your toothbrush; how could you make it better? Discuss with someone else what your improvement would be and the difference it would make when cleaning your teeth.

Tell someone what you have eaten today and which of the foods are best for your teeth.

Helping plants grow well: light (part one)

Aim of the activity

- To explore the importance of light for growth in green plants.

Cover a small patch of grass with something solid that won't let light through. (Make sure you check with an adult where it would be okay to do this!)

Think about and discuss

What do you think will happen to the grass? What else might change under the cover?

Note for teachers

You may need to cater for those without access to grass.

Helping plants grow well: light (part two)

Aim of the activity

- To review the appearance of your covered grass and to consider the importance of light for growth in green plants.

Remove the cover from your patch of grass and look carefully at your findings.

Think about and discuss

What has happened to the grass? Discuss with someone else some reasons for any changes you see. Did anything else change under the cover? If so, what?

Leave the grass uncovered now. What do you think will happen?

Helping plants grow well: growth

Aim of the activity

- To explore what happens to roots and shoots when a bean seed germinates.

Roll up some newspaper and place it in a see-through pot. Now push your bean down the side (between the newspaper and the edge of the pot), making sure you can see it clearly. Now wash your hands.

Add a couple of centimetres of water to the pot and check every day that the newspaper is still damp. Add a little more water if needed.

Think about and discuss

What did you notice? Discuss your findings and ideas with someone else.

Note for teachers

You will need to warn children in advance to save a see-through plastic container for this activity. Provide each child with a broad bean and remind children to wash their hands, as beans are often treated with fungicide.

Devising an investigation: the best temperature for growth

Aim of the activity

- To think carefully about planning a fair test.

Think about and discuss

How could you test to find out what is the best temperature for growing plants? (You don't need to carry out your plan.)

You need to make sure you plan a fair test. Think about:

- how you could make measurements
- how you could decide which is the best temperature.

Fair test, mmmmm

Tell someone how you will ensure it is a fair test.

If you want to, and have time, carry out your investigation.

Note for parents

In a 'fair test', it is important to keep all the aspects of the investigation the same, apart from the one being investigated. For example, if you want to find out whether light or dark conditions are best for plant growth, you should try to find a light place and a dark place that are about the same temperature. If you put one in the fridge it would be both dark and cold, and it would be impossible to know whether it was the light levels or the temperature differences that affected plant growth the most.

Moving and growing: bones

Aim of the activity

- To examine the nature of bones and their function.

Feel the bones in your arm and hand; think about what they look like and draw your ideas on the outline below.

squeeze

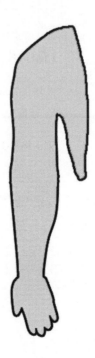

Think about and discuss

Show your sketch to someone else and explain your choices of bone shape, size and position. What words can you use to describe your bones? Do you have any other questions?

Feel the bones that make up your ribcage. Can you feel the ribs go around your body?

Tell someone how your ribcage feels. Do you know what it protects?

Moving and growing: muscles and joints

Aim of the activity

- To think about what muscles do.

Move your fingers and watch what happens under the skin in your hand and your forearm.

Feel your calf muscles while you wriggle your foot.

Think about and discuss

Describe and discuss how your muscles feel and any things that you notice about their movement. Try to describe and explain what is happening to your muscles when you move your arm or leg.

Habitats: plants

Aim of the activity

- To consider the importance of plants in our lives.

Predict how many things you used and ate today that came from plants. Make a list of all the things you can think of.

 ## Think about and discuss

Does your list contain more or less than you predicted? Are there any items that puzzle or surprise you?

Habitats: food chains

Choose one type of food you have eaten today and think about where it originally came from. If it's an animal, think about where its food originally came from.

Use your chosen food to create a food chain. How many links does it have?

Note for parents

The arrows on a food chain point from the plant or animal being eaten to the animal doing the eating.

Debate: is it a good thing to keep animals in zoos or wildlife parks?

Aim of the activity

- To consider the advantages and disadvantages of zoos.

Think about and discuss

- What are the benefits of zoos or wildlife parks?
- What are the disadvantages?

Decide which of the two statements below you most agree with, and prepare a one-minute speech to explain why.

It is a good thing to keep animals in zoos or wildlife parks.
It is not a good thing to keep animals in zoos or wildlife parks.

Life and living processes

Keeping healthy: food types

Aim of the activity

- To think about food types and their purpose.

Think about a meal you have eaten today
and the different foods it contained.

 ## Think about and discuss

Decide which foods gave you energy that would be used to help you grow and
which foods would be used to keep you healthy.

Keeping healthy: breakfast cereals

Aim of the activity

- To compare the nutritional content of breakfast cereals.

Look at the nutritional content of two or three different breakfast cereals.

Think about and discuss

How would you decide which breakfast cereal is the healthiest and gives you the best start to the day?

Keeping healthy: exercise

Aim of the activity

- To explore heart rate.

Take the pulse of someone you know and work out how many times their heart beats in one minute. Ask your volunteer to jog or jump on the spot for one minute and then take their pulse again.

Work out how many times their heart beats in one minute, straight after the exercise.

Think about and discuss

Describe to your volunteer what happened to their pulse and heart rate. Think about why this happened and discuss what was going on inside their body.

Debate: which is most important – a healthy diet or taking regular exercise?

Aim of the activity

- To consider the advantages of a healthy diet and taking regular exercise.

Think about and discuss

- What are the benefits of eating healthily?
- What are the benefits of taking regular exercise?

Decide which of the two statements below you most agree with, and prepare a one-minute speech to explain why.

It is more important to eat healthily than take regular exercise.

It is more important to take regular exercise than eat healthily.

Lifecycles (plants): flowers

Aim of the activity

- To get to know flowering plants and their life processes.

Look closely at a flower such as blossom on a fruit tree, lily or geranium. Can you see the different parts of the flower?

 Tell someone what some of the parts of the flower are for. What might happen if you took one of the parts of the flower away?

 ## Note for teachers

You will need to time this activity carefully!

Lifecycles (plants): germination

Aim of the activity

- To explore germination.

Roll up some newspaper and place it in a see-through pot. Now push your bean down the side (between the newspaper and the edge of the pot), making sure you can see it clearly. Add enough water to make the newspaper damp. Now wash your hands. Put your pot in a dark cupboard.

Add a couple of centimetres of water to the pot and check every day that the newspaper is still damp. Add a little more water if needed.

 ## Think about and discuss

Describe to someone what happened to your bean whilst it was in the dark cupboard. Was this what you expected? What other investigations could you try?

Lifecycles (plants): seeds

Aim of the activity

- To think about why plants have seeds.

Think about all the seeds you have eaten today. How many can you think of?

 Tell someone the number of seeds you have eaten today and talk about any you are unsure of. What would happen if plants did not have seeds?

Lifecycles (plants): seed dispersal

Aim of the activity

- To think about what seeds need to be dispersed.

Think about and discuss

Describe the special things that different seeds need so they can move from their parent plant to a new place. Think about the shape and the parts of the seed and how these help it travel.

Decide what you think is the best feature any seed has that helps it travel and explain why.

Invent a new seed design and sketch it below. What features does your seed have and how does this help it travel?

Interdependence and adaptation

 Tell someone ways in which a polar bear is adapted to life in the Arctic.

 ## Think about and discuss

If polar bears were to survive in a warmer world, how might they need to adapt? Discuss some features the species would need to develop or lose in order to survive.

What would it be like to try and live on the planet Mars?

Create an alien that could live on Mars. Think about the features it would need to live and survive. Explain your choices about your alien to someone else.

Micro-organisms: types of microbes

Aim of the activity

- To think about the uses of microbes.

 **TRY THIS!**

Check your fridge and food cupboards. Can you find any foods that are micro-organisms or that contain micro-organisms?

 ## Think about and discuss

Discuss these true/false statements:

All bacteria are bad.
You should always use soap when washing your hands.
Bacteria help to break down food scraps and leaves in a compost heap.
Bread without yeast will rise.

Create your own true/false statement about micro-organisms to test your class.

Micro-organisms: your questions

 Tell someone everything you know about micro-organisms (e.g. bacteria, viruses, fungi).

 Tell someone any questions you have, and ask them if they have any questions.

Think about and discuss

Choose your favourite question to share with your class; you don't need to know the answer!

Micro-organisms: composting

Aim of the activity

• To explore decomposition.

Think about a meal you have eaten today. What parts of your meal could be composted?

 Tell someone all the things that could be composted from your meal.

Think about and discuss

 Discuss what happens when the food is left to decompose and why composting is important.

Devising an investigation: best conditions for compost

Aim of the activity

- To think carefully about planning a fair test.

Think about and discuss

How could you test to find out the best conditions for kitchen scraps and garden waste to compost?

You will need to make sure you plan a fair test, and think about how you could make measurements or observations upon which to base your conclusions.

Tell someone how you will ensure it is a fair test.

If you want to, and have time, carry out your investigation.

Note for parents

In a 'fair test', it is important to keep all the aspects of the investigation the same, apart from the one being investigated.

Materials and their properties

Characteristics of materials: what would you use?

Aim of the activity

- To explore the properties of different materials (e.g. wood, metal, paper, fabric) that make them suitable (or unsuitable!) for use in creating certain objects.

Find a few household objects (e.g. fork, chair, margarine pot) and tell someone what each one is made of and why you think it is made of that material.

 ## Think about and discuss

What materials **wouldn't** you use to make a blanket? Or a table, or a door, or a towel ...

Why not?

Rocks and soils: house materials

Aim of the activity

- To explore the properties of materials used to build houses.

Look closely at the bricks or material your house is made of.

Think about and discuss

What are the bricks made of, do you think? Can you find any other materials that seem to have similar ingredients?

Why are houses made of stone, brick or concrete, etc.? Why aren't houses made of jelly?

What else wouldn't you build a house from?

Rocks and soils: erosion

Aim of the activity

- To explore the causes of erosion.

Outside, look for places where rocks, bricks, concrete or soil have been worn away. You may have to look very carefully.

 Tell someone what you think has caused this erosion.

 ## Think about and discuss

If you could see some rock or soil that had been worn away, where is the worn away stuff now?

Rocks and soils: volcanoes

Aim of the activity

- To share as much knowledge about volcanoes as possible.

Tell someone everything you know about volcanoes.

Ask someone to tell you everything they know about volcanoes.

 ## Think about and discuss

What questions do you have about volcanoes that you would still like to find out the answers to?

Devising an investigation: strongest rock

Aim of the activity

- To think about how to set up a fair test.

Think about and discuss

If you wanted to know which kind of rock was strongest, how could you plan a fair test to find out? (You don't need to try it, just decide how you would do it.)

You will need to think about all the ways in which you will make sure it is a fair test, and what measurements or observations you will need to make in order to decide which rock was the strongest.

Note for parents

In a 'fair test', it is important to keep all the aspects of the investigation the same, apart from the one being investigated.

Keeping warm (thermal insulators): comparing materials

Aim of the activity

• To explore the thermal insulating qualities of different materials.

Put one ice cube on a plastic or wooden board and one on a metal baking sheet and see what happens.

Remember, to ensure it is a fair test, make sure you use an ice cube of about the same size on each board and have the boards in the same place; don't touch the ice cubes once you've got them on the boards.

Think about and discuss

Which ice cube melts first? What does this tell you about the thermal insulation qualities of the different materials?

Note for parents

The term 'material' relates to all kinds of stuff, not just fabrics.

Keeping warm (thermal insulators): slowing the transfer of heat energy

Aim of the activity

- To explore how the transfer of energy can be slowed by a thermal insulator.

Take eight ice cubes and two plastic bags; put four ice cubes in each bag. Put both bags on a table and then cover one bag with a jumper or a towel.

Think about and discuss

Which ice cubes melt most quickly, those covered by the jumper/towel or those with no cover?

Keeping warm (thermal insulators): insulation in the home

Aim of the activity

- To explore the use of thermal insulators in everyday life.

Active fact

A thermal insulator prevents or slows the transfer of heat energy.

Think about and discuss

When you take something hot from the oven, why do you use an oven glove? What energy transfer does the oven glove slow or prevent?

Look for, or think of, other thermal insulators in the home. Here are a couple to get you started:

- most pan handles are made from wood or plastic
- you probably have a thermal insulator on your bed.

Think about and discuss

In each case, what energy transfer is being slowed or prevented?

Solids, liquids and separating: teabags and sieving?

Think about and discuss

How does a teabag work?

Ask your parent/carer if you can cut open a teabag to have a look inside.

 ## Think about and discuss

How does the water get in and out of the teabag, while the tea leaves stay inside?

Find two substances in your kitchen that can be mixed then separated by sieving.

Solids, liquids and separating: sieving

Aim of the activity

• To explore which materials, when mixed with water, can be separated by sieving.

If you added a tablespoon of each of these solids to a pan full of cold water and stirred for one or two minutes, what would happen in each case?

• flour
• sugar
• rice
• pasta.

Try out any that you are unsure of.

 ## Think about and discuss

Would you be able to get back any of these by sieving? If not, how would you go about retrieving them?

Materials and their properties

Gases around us: gases you know

Take a deep breath. Hold it for a few seconds, then breathe out.

Tell someone how many gases you have just breathed in.

Think about and discuss

How was the air you breathed out different from the air you breathed in?

Take it in turns with someone to name a different gas each time. How many can you think of? Do you know where you might find each gas?

Gases around us: is air real stuff?

Aim of the activity

- To explore whether air has mass.

Think about and discuss

Does air weigh anything?

Could you invent a way in which you could weigh air?

Think about and discuss

A challenging question: why doesn't air drift off into space?

Debate: driving versus using the bus

Aim of the activity

- To consider the benefits and disadvantages of travelling by car or bus.

Think about and discuss

- What are the benefits of travelling by car?
- What are the benefits of travelling by bus?

Decide which of the two statements below you most agree with, and prepare a one-minute speech to explain why.

It is better to travel by car than by bus.
It is better to travel by bus than by car.

Changing state: liquid and gas

Aim of the activity

- To explore the changes of state from gas to liquid and from liquid to gas.

Breathe on a cold window. Watch what happens to the patch where you breathed.

 Tell someone what happened when you breathed on the glass and what happened next.

Take a cold bottle (e.g. a milk bottle) out of the fridge and leave it to stand for a few minutes. Run your finger up the side; what do you notice?

 Tell someone what you notice when you run your finger up the side of the cold bottle.

Changing state: solid and liquid

Aim of the activity

- To explore the changes of state from solid to liquid and from liquid to solid.

Take three plastic cups (yoghurt pots or any small containers will do, so long as they are the same size and shape). Put one ice cube in the first pot, two in the second and three in the third. Put them all in the same place.

Think about and discuss

Which ice cube(s) will melt first? Will the number of ice cubes in a pot affect the time it takes for them to melt?

Look again at the pots; what happened?

Think about and discuss

If you put them in the freezer, which pot of water would take the longest to freeze?

Changing state: evaporation

Aim of the activity

- To consider the best conditions for evaporation to occur.

If you put 10 ml of water in a tall, thin jar and 10 ml of water in a shallow, wide jar, and left them both in the same place, which do you think would evaporate most quickly?

Take two pieces of kitchen roll (or tissue) and pour the same amount of water on each (two teaspoons should be enough). Now fold one and leave one flat and leave them both in the same place. Which dries quickest?

Think about and discuss

What are all the factors that affect how quickly evaporation takes place?

A challenging question: is there a difference between evaporation and boiling?

Dissolving: mixing solids with water

Aim of the activity

- To explore which solids dissolve.

Use three similar-sized beakers and half-fill each with water. Add two teaspoons of salt to the first beaker and stir. Observe carefully what happens and describe it to someone.

Add two teaspoons of flour to the second beaker and two teaspoons of sugar to the third; stir them both.

Think about and discuss

How were the materials different when you mixed them with the water. Which dissolved?

As an extra challenge, try mixing some other materials with water and observing what happens.

Note for parents

Try to avoid your child asking why one material dissolved and another didn't unless you know the answer.

Dissolving: reversing the process

Aim of the activity

- To explore the reversibility of dissolving.

Half-fill a beaker with water, add five or six teaspoons of salt or sugar and stir well. When all the salt or sugar has dissolved, put four or five teaspoons of the solution into a shallow tray (a small tin-foil case or similar would be ideal). If you have some, add two or three drops of food colouring to this small amount of liquid and stir it in. Find somewhere safe to leave the shallow tray.

Think about and discuss

What do you think will happen? Check the tray every few hours and observe what is happening.

Tell someone what happens.

Devising an investigation: best conditions for dissolving

Aim of the activity

- To think carefully about planning a fair test.

Think about and discuss

How could you test to find out the best conditions for dissolving sugar in water? Try to think of all the variables that could be changed during the investigation.

You will need to make sure you plan a fair test, and think about how you could make measurements or observations upon which to base your conclusions.

Tell someone how you will ensure it is a fair test.

If you want to, and if you have time, carry out your investigation.

 Warning! If you want to use hot water, ask an adult to help.

Note for parents

In a 'fair test', it is important to keep all the aspects of the investigation the same, apart from the one being investigated.

Reversible and non-reversible change: mixing and heating

Aim of the activity

- To explore reversible and non-reversible changes.

Put two or three teaspoons of vinegar in a beaker. Add a teaspoon of bicarbonate of soda and observe what happens.

Think about and discuss

Is this change a reversible or non-reversible change?

Toast a slice of bread. In how many ways has the bread changed? Are these reversible or non-reversible changes?

Think about and discuss

How many reversible and non-reversible changes are involved in your everyday life (e.g. cooking, clothing, transport, etc.)?

Reversible and non-reversible change: your questions

Aim of the activity

- To think of questions related to reversible and non-reversible changes.

Think about and discuss

Tell someone everything you know about reversible and non-reversible changes.

Tell someone any questions you have, and ask them if they have any questions.

Choose your favourite question to share with your class; you don't need to know the answer!

Reversible and non-reversible change: the water cycle

Aim of the activity

- To think about the water cycle and where our water comes from.

Drink a glass of water.

Think about and discuss

Where does your water come from?

Tell someone everything you know about the water cycle.

Where will the water you drank go next on its journey?

Physical processes

Magnets and springs: true and false

Aim of the activity

- To discuss what we know about magnets and springs.

Think about the following statements and decide if they are true or false:

All metals are magnetic.
Some magnets can be turned on and off.
All springs are designed to push.

Think about and discuss

Are magnets and springs similar in any ways?

Magnets and springs: paper springs

Take a sheet of paper and cut it into strips. Take two strips and hold them together, one end on the other, at right angles to each other. Fold the bottom one over the top one, and repeat.

Think about and discuss

How could you make the paper spring better? How could you test which paper spring was best?

Magnets and springs: searching for magnets and springs at home

Aim of the activity

- To explore the role of magnets and springs in everyday life.

 **TRY THIS!**

Ask your parent/carer if you can take apart a **cheap** click-action ball-point pen. Use a tray to collect any parts that fall out. Is there a spring inside the pen?

 ## Think about and discuss

Why does the pen have a spring inside? If you put the pen back together, can you feel the push of the spring?

 Tell someone everything you know about magnets and how they are used in everyday life.

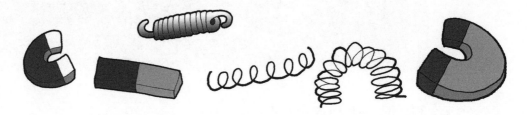

 ## Note for parents

The fridge door probably has ground-up magnets in the rubber edging to help make an airtight seal around the door.

Light and shadows: opaque, translucent and transparent

Aim of the activity

- To explore how much light passes through different materials.

 Tell someone, if you can, what these words mean:

- opaque
- translucent
- transparent.

Find some objects in your house that are opaque, some that are translucent and some that are transparent. Try these two tests to see how much light travels through them:

1   Using a lamp or torch, use each object to cast a shadow on a wall. Which objects cast the darkest or clearest shadows?
2   Try to look through the objects. What can you see? Does any light pass through each one?

Think about and discuss

 Do the two tests give the same results?

Light and shadows: changing shadows

Aim of the activity

- To explore how shadows are made and how they can be changed.

 Tell someone how shadows are formed and anything else you know about shadows.

Using a torch or a room lamp (or sunshine) make as many different shape shadows as you can using the same object (for example, a plastic plate).

Try to change the size of the shadow

Think about and discuss

 Can you come up with a general rule to describe how the size of a shadow changes depending on where it is in relation to the light source or the surface it is on?

 Ask someone if they have any questions about light and shadows. Do you have any?

Friction: slipping and gripping

Find a coin and lay it flat on a table. Give it a gentle flick or push and see how far it travels. Now try giving it a similar flick on a different surface (e.g. carpet, wood flooring) and see how far it travels.

Think about and discuss

Does the coin slide equally well across all surfaces? Which surface has the most friction and which the least?

Can you think of a time when it is good to have a lot of friction?

Friction: reducing friction

Aim of the activity

- To explore how friction can be reduced.

Think about and discuss

Look at or think about a bicycle.

- Why do we oil some parts on a bike?
- Which parts of the bike is it a good idea to oil regularly?
- Which parts would it not be a good idea to oil at all?

Physical processes

Earth, Sun, Moon: day and night

Aim of the activity

- To explore how day and night occur.

Take a torch and a spherical object (an apple, orange or tennis ball would do) into a darkish room. Shine the torch on the ball and slowly rotate it on the spot to show someone how day turns to night.

Think about and discuss

Does everyone have night-time at the same time? When it is midday in England, what time is it in Australia?

Do you have any questions of your own about day and night?

Note for teachers

It is recommended that you use this exercise only after modelling day and night in class.

Earth, Sun, Moon: phases of the Moon

Aim of the activity

- To explore how the phases of the moon occur.

Ask someone why the Moon seems to be different shapes at different times.

Take a torch and a spherical object (an apple, orange or tennis ball would do) into a darkish room. Hold the ball at arm's length, just above head height, and ask someone to shine the torch on the ball. Now shuffle your feet so you turn slowly anti-clockwise, keeping the torch directed at the ball as it moves around with you.

Now swap over so that you hold the torch and someone else holds the ball.

Think about and discuss

How long is one lunar (moon) cycle?

What other questions do you have about the moon?

Note for teachers

It is recommended that you use this exercise only after modelling the phases of the moon in class.

Debate: is space exploration good use of money?

Think about and discuss

How has mankind benefited from space exploration? Think about:

- putting some men on the moon
- making the International Space Station
- creating the Hubble telescope, which can see into deep space
- sending probes to Mars.

What else could the money have been spent on? Consider:

- hospitals
- famine relief
- schools.

Decide which of the two statements below you most agree with, and prepare a one-minute speech to explain why.

Space exploration is good use of money.
Space exploration is not good use of money.

Changing sounds: sound travels

Tie about five spoons and forks onto a 1-metre length of string. Push the string firmly onto the front of your ear, so that your ears are both completely closed to the air, with the string making a good contact with your closed ear. Swing your head so that the spoons and forks jangle together.

Think about and discuss

How do the spoons and forks sound? How does the sound get from them to your ears? Do they sound different if you jangle them with your ears open?

Put your head down sideways on a table so that you can press your ear to the surface. Gently tap the table-top.

 Warning! Make sure you only tap the table-top gently!

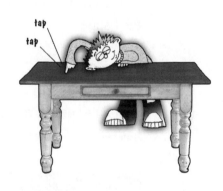

Think about and discuss

Is the sound loudest when it travels through the air or through the solid table?

Next time you have a bath, lie down with your ears submerged. What can you hear? Try tapping the sides of the bath, above the water and below the water. Try humming or singing to yourself.

How are the sounds different when your ears are in the water, compared with when they are not? Is the sound loudest when it travels through the air or through the water?

Changing sounds: sound travels more slowly than light

Aim of the activity

•   To explore the fact that sound and light travel at different speeds.

Look out for fireworks during the dark evenings in November. Try to notice very carefully whether you see the flash and hear the bang at exactly the same moment.

Think about and discuss

When a firework goes off, do you see the flash or hear the bang first?

If the firework is further away, does this make a difference to the gap between the flash and the bang?

Next time there is a thunder storm, watch and listen for the gap between the flash of the lightning and the rumble of the thunder.

Think about and discuss

Can you tell if the thunderstorm is getting closer or moving further away by timing the gap between the flash of the lightning and the rumble of the thunder?

Changing sounds: directing and collecting sounds

Aim of the activity

- To explore how sounds travel through air and how sounds can be funnelled.

Take a piece of paper (A4 or larger), roll it into a cone and tape it lightly closed with some tape. Try using it like a megaphone or like an ear-trumpet.

Think about and discuss

How does the paper cone change the sounds when speaking and listening? Is the way the sound travels changed?

Make another paper cone and use one for speaking into and one for listening. Use the cones to whisper a message to someone else across the room.

whisper whisper

Think about and discuss

What happens when you change the size of the cone or the size of the hole at each end? How can you change your cone to make it better for listening or speaking?

Changing sounds: changing pitch

Aim of the activity

- To explore how the pitch of sounds can be changed.

Find a bottle, a teaspoon and a jug. Pour some water into the bottle and tap it with the teaspoon. Now ask someone to slowly pour more water into the bottle while you keep on tapping.

Think about and discuss

How does the pitch change as you pour the water in? Does it get higher or lower? Think of some musical instruments in the same musical family (e.g. violin, viola, cello, double bass); can you complete this general rule about how the size of an instrument affects its pitch? For example, 'The bigger the instrument the . . .'

Forces in action: building structures

Aim of the activity

- To explore the impact of shape in structural strength.

 **TRY THIS!**

Find someone to challenge to a building competition, or to work together with you. The challenge is to build the tallest free-standing structure you can, using limited materials.

Each person should have:

- 10 sheets of newspaper, or 15 sheets of scrap A4 paper
- some masking tape or other sticky tape (about 1 metre in total).

Your structure should not be stuck to the floor or table and should not lean against anything else; it should stand up on its own.

Plan first, then get building.

 ## Think about and discuss

What were the most successful elements of your structure? How could you improve it? What thinking skills did you use when doing the planning and building?

Forces in action: friction in sport

Aim of the activity

- To explore how friction is important in many sports, and a lack of friction is important in others.

Active fact

Runners who compete in sprinting events use spikes on the soles of their running shoes to give them extra grip (increased friction) on the track.

Think about and discuss

How do people in other sports try to increase friction in different situations, e.g. footballers, goalkeepers, mountain bikers, ice climbers.

In which sports is it important to reduce friction as much as possible (don't forget that air resistance is also a form of friction)? How do sports people try to reduce friction?

Forces in action: a thought experiment

Aim of the activity

•   To think of air resistance as a force.

Imagine you have just jumped out of an aeroplane flying high in the atmosphere. You are free-falling; you haven't opened your parachute yet. Imagine the air rushing past you with your arms and legs out wide. Now imagine that all of the air suddenly disappears. How would this change your fall to Earth? What would happen if you tried to open your parachute?

Think about and discuss

What questions do you have about what else might change if the air suddenly disappeared?

Devising an investigation: shoe with the best grip

Aim of the activity

*   To think carefully about planning a fair test.

Think about and discuss

How could you test to see which one of your shoes has the most grip? You will need to make sure you plan a fair test, and think about how you could make measurements or observations upon which to base your conclusions.

Tell someone how you will ensure it is a fair test.

If you have time, carry out your investigation.

Note for parents

In a 'fair test', it is important to keep all the aspects of the investigation the same, apart from the one being investigated.

How we see things: reflected light

Aim of the activity

- To explore the idea that everything we see reflects light.

Active fact

We all know we need light to see things, but did you know that everything we see is reflecting light?

Take a torch and some objects of different colours (coloured paper, books, etc.). Shine the torch onto one of the objects; see if you can reflect any light from the object onto a white wall or reflect the light onto someone's face, and make them glow.

 Warning! Be careful to make sure you don't shine the torch into anyone's eyes.

See if you can reflect light off your hand, or your jumper/shirt.

Think about and discuss

Which colours reflected the most light? Which were the least good at reflecting light?

How we see things: pupils responding to light

Have a good look at someone else's eye, and compare your own by looking in a mirror. Look closely at the pupil, the black circle in the middle of the eye.

Ask the other person to cover their eyes with their hands for about 20 seconds. When they take their hands away, look again very closely at the pupils. What do you notice?

Stand very close to a mirror and look at your pupils. Now put your hands up beside your head so that less light reaches your face. Look carefully at your pupils. What do you notice?

Think about and discuss

When are pupils at their largest? Why do you think this is?

How we see things: your questions

Aim of the activity

- To think of questions related to light, colour and how we see things.

 Tell someone everything you know about light, colour and how we see things.

Ask someone any questions you have, and ask them if they have any questions.

Choose your favourite question to share with your class; you don't need to know the answer!